EMMANUEL JOSEPH

Echoes of Yesterday, How Nostalgia and Curiosity Fuel Resilience in a Digital Age

Copyright © 2025 by Emmanuel Joseph

All rights reserved. No part of this publication may be reproduced, stored or transmitted in any form or by any means, electronic, mechanical, photocopying, recording, scanning, or otherwise without written permission from the publisher. It is illegal to copy this book, post it to a website, or distribute it by any other means without permission.

First edition

This book was professionally typeset on Reedsy. Find out more at reedsy.com

Contents

1	Chapter 1: The Echoes of Yesterday	1
2	Chapter 2: The Curious Mind	3
3	Chapter 3: The Intersection of Nostalgia and Curiosity	5
4	Chapter 4: The Power of Storytelling	7
5	Chapter 5: The Digital Archive	9
6	Chapter 6: The Resilient Mindset	11
7	Chapter 7: The Role of Technology	13
8	Chapter 8: The Power of Connection	15
9	Chapter 9: The Journey of Self-Discovery	17
10	Chapter 10: The Art of Adaptation	19
11	Chapter 11: The Impact of Social Media	21
12	Chapter 12: The Role of Mindfulness	23
13	Chapter 13: The Art of Reflection	25
14	Chapter 14: The Influence of Culture	27
15	Chapter 16: Embracing Change	29
16	Chapter 17: The Future of Resilience	31

1

Chapter 1: The Echoes of Yesterday

Nostalgia is a powerful force that has the capacity to transport us back to moments long gone. It stirs up memories of times when life seemed simpler, filled with joy and wonder. These echoes of yesterday remind us of our roots and shape our identity, helping us understand who we are today. By reflecting on our past experiences, we gain insights into our strengths and vulnerabilities, which ultimately fuels our resilience. Embracing nostalgia allows us to appreciate the journey we've taken and prepares us to face future challenges with a stronger sense of self.

Nostalgia isn't just about reminiscing; it's also about learning from our past. By revisiting old memories, we can analyze the choices we made and the lessons we learned. This process of introspection enables us to identify patterns in our behavior and recognize areas for growth. As we gain a deeper understanding of our past, we become more equipped to navigate the complexities of the digital age, where change is constant and the pressure to adapt is ever-present.

The digital age has given us unprecedented access to our past, with social media platforms and digital archives preserving our memories in ways that were once unimaginable. This constant connection to our history allows us to draw strength from the experiences we've shared with others, fostering a sense of continuity and belonging. By embracing the echoes of yesterday, we can harness the power of nostalgia to build a more resilient and adaptive mindset.

In this fast-paced world, it's easy to feel disconnected from our roots. However, by nurturing our connection to the past, we can ground ourselves in a sense of continuity and stability. Nostalgia serves as a reminder that we are part of a larger narrative, one that stretches across time and space. By embracing our history and learning from it, we can build a foundation of resilience that will support us as we navigate the challenges of the digital age.

2

Chapter 2: The Curious Mind

Curiosity is a driving force that propels us to explore the unknown and seek out new experiences. It is the spark that ignites our desire to learn, grow, and evolve. In a digital age where information is abundant and easily accessible, curiosity becomes an essential tool for navigating the vast landscape of knowledge. By cultivating a curious mindset, we open ourselves up to new possibilities and opportunities for growth.

A curious mind is not content with the status quo; it constantly seeks out new challenges and experiences. This relentless pursuit of knowledge and understanding helps us develop a deeper appreciation for the world around us. As we explore new ideas and perspectives, we become more adaptable and resilient in the face of change. Curiosity drives us to question our assumptions and push the boundaries of our comfort zones, ultimately fostering a mindset of growth and resilience.

In the digital age, curiosity is more important than ever. The rapid pace of technological advancements and the ever-evolving landscape of information require us to be constantly learning and adapting. By nurturing our curiosity, we can stay ahead of the curve and remain relevant in an increasingly complex world. A curious mind is always open to new ideas and ready to embrace change, making it a powerful tool for building resilience.

Curiosity also fosters creativity and innovation. When we approach the world with a sense of wonder and inquisitiveness, we are more likely to come up with novel solutions to problems and discover new ways of doing things. This creative mindset is essential for thriving in a digital age where change is constant and adaptability is key. By cultivating our curiosity, we can unlock our potential for growth and resilience, allowing us to navigate the challenges of the modern world with confidence and grace.

3

Chapter 3: The Intersection of Nostalgia and Curiosity

Nostalgia and curiosity may seem like opposing forces, but they are in fact deeply interconnected. While nostalgia roots us in our past, curiosity propels us forward into the unknown. Together, they create a dynamic interplay that fuels our resilience and adaptability. By embracing both the echoes of yesterday and the wonders of tomorrow, we can develop a more holistic and balanced approach to life.

At the heart of this intersection lies a profound sense of self-awareness. By reflecting on our past experiences and exploring new possibilities, we gain a deeper understanding of who we are and what drives us. This self-awareness is crucial for building resilience, as it allows us to recognize our strengths and weaknesses, and to navigate the challenges of the digital age with greater clarity and confidence.

Nostalgia and curiosity also work together to foster a sense of continuity and connection. While nostalgia reminds us of our roots and the relationships we've built, curiosity encourages us to forge new connections and create new memories. This balance between the past and the future helps us maintain a sense of stability and belonging, even in the face of rapid change.

By embracing both nostalgia and curiosity, we can develop a more resilient mindset that is better equipped to handle the uncertainties of the digital age. Nostalgia provides us with a sense of grounding and continuity, while curiosity drives us to explore new possibilities and adapt to change. Together, they create a powerful foundation for growth and resilience, allowing us to navigate the complexities of the modern world with confidence and grace.

4

Chapter 4: The Power of Storytelling

Storytelling is a powerful tool that allows us to connect with others and make sense of our experiences. Through stories, we can share our memories, explore our curiosities, and build a sense of community and belonging. In the digital age, storytelling has taken on new forms and dimensions, with social media platforms and digital content providing us with endless opportunities to share our narratives.

Nostalgia often plays a central role in storytelling, as it allows us to revisit and reflect on our past experiences. By sharing our memories with others, we can create a sense of connection and understanding, fostering empathy and compassion. These shared experiences can serve as a source of strength and resilience, reminding us that we are not alone in our struggles and triumphs.

Curiosity, on the other hand, drives us to explore new stories and perspectives. It encourages us to seek out diverse voices and experiences, broadening our understanding of the world around us. By embracing curiosity in our storytelling, we can foster a more inclusive and open-minded approach to life, building bridges between different cultures and communities.

In the digital age, storytelling has the potential to amplify our resilience by connecting us with a global audience. By sharing our narratives and engaging with others, we can create a sense of solidarity and support that transcends geographical boundaries. Through the power of storytelling, we can harness the forces of nostalgia and curiosity to build a more resilient and connected world.

5

Chapter 5: The Digital Archive

The digital age has given us unprecedented access to our memories, with countless photos, videos, and messages preserved in the vast expanse of the internet. This digital archive allows us to revisit our past experiences and draw strength from the memories we've created. By engaging with our digital history, we can cultivate a sense of continuity and connection that fuels our resilience.

Nostalgia plays a significant role in our engagement with the digital archive, as it allows us to reflect on the moments that have shaped our lives. By revisiting old photos and messages, we can relive the joy and wonder of our past experiences, reminding us of the strength and resilience we've demonstrated in the face of adversity.

Curiosity, on the other hand, drives us to explore new ways of preserving and sharing our memories. The digital age has given rise to innovative platforms and technologies that allow us to document our lives in ways that were once unimaginable. By embracing these new tools, we can create a rich tapestry of memories that reflects the diversity and complexity of our experiences.

The digital archive also fosters a sense of connection and belonging, as it allows us to share our memories with others and engage with their stories. By creating a collective narrative that spans time and space, we can build a sense of community and support that transcends geographical boundaries.

This shared history serves as a powerful foundation for resilience, reminding us that we are part of a larger narrative that stretches across time and space.

6

Chapter 6: The Resilient Mindset

Resilience is the ability to adapt and thrive in the face of adversity. It is a skill that can be cultivated through the interplay of nostalgia and curiosity, as we learn from our past experiences and explore new possibilities. By developing a resilient mindset, we can navigate the challenges of the digital age with greater confidence and grace.

Nostalgia helps us build resilience by reminding us of the strength and perseverance we've demonstrated in the past. By reflecting on our past experiences, we can gain insights into our strengths and vulnerabilities, allowing us to approach future challenges with a greater sense of self-awareness and confidence. Nostalgia also fosters a sense of continuity and connection, reminding us that we are part of a larger narrative that stretches across time and space.

Curiosity, on the other hand, drives us to explore new possibilities and embrace change. By approaching the world with a sense of wonder and inquisitiveness, we can develop a growth mindset that allows us to adapt and thrive in the face of adversity. Curiosity encourages us to question our assumptions and push the boundaries of our comfort zones, ultimately fostering a mindset of growth and resilience.

By embracing both nostalgia and curiosity, we can develop a resilient mindset that is better equipped to handle the uncertainties of the digital age. Nostalgia provides us with a sense of grounding and continuity, while curiosity drives us to explore new possibilities and adapt to change. Together, they create a powerful foundation for growth and resilience, allowing us to navigate the complexities of the modern world with confidence and grace.

7

Chapter 7: The Role of Technology

Technology plays a significant role in shaping our experiences of nostalgia and curiosity. The digital age has given us unprecedented access to our memories and the world around us, allowing us to engage with our past and explore new possibilities in ways that were once unimaginable. By understanding the role of technology in our lives, we can harness its potential to build resilience and adaptability.

Nostalgia is often fueled by the digital archive, with social media platforms and digital content preserving our memories in ways that were once unimaginable. This constant connection to our past allows us to draw strength from our experiences and foster a sense of continuity and belonging. By engaging with our digital history, we can cultivate a sense of grounding and stability that helps us navigate the challenges of the digital age.

Curiosity, on the other hand, is driven by the vast landscape of knowledge available at our fingertips. The digital age has given us unprecedented access to information, allowing us to explore new ideas and perspectives with ease. By nurturing our curiosity, we can stay ahead of the curve and remain relevant in an increasingly complex world. Technology serves as a powerful tool for fostering curiosity and innovation, driving us to push the boundaries of our understanding and adapt to change.

By embracing the role of technology in our lives, we can harness its potential to build resilience and adaptability. Nostalgia and curiosity, fueled by the digital archive and the vast landscape of knowledge, create a powerful foundation for growth and resilience. By understanding the interplay between technology, nostalgia, and curiosity, we can navigate the complexities of the digital age with confidence and grace.

8

Chapter 8: The Power of Connection

Connection is a fundamental aspect of the human experience, and it plays a crucial role in our resilience and adaptability. In the digital age, technology has transformed the way we connect with others, enabling us to build and maintain relationships across vast distances. By fostering meaningful connections, we can create a support network that helps us navigate the challenges of the modern world.

Nostalgia often strengthens our connections with others, as it allows us to share our memories and experiences. By reminiscing about the past, we can create a sense of continuity and belonging, fostering empathy and understanding. These shared experiences serve as a source of strength and resilience, reminding us that we are not alone in our struggles and triumphs.

Curiosity, on the other hand, drives us to seek out new connections and explore diverse perspectives. By engaging with others and embracing different viewpoints, we can broaden our understanding of the world around us. This openness to new ideas and experiences fosters a sense of adaptability and resilience, allowing us to navigate the complexities of the digital age with greater ease.

In the digital age, technology provides us with endless opportunities to connect with others and build meaningful relationships. By leveraging the power of technology, we can create a support network that helps us navigate the challenges of the modern world. Through the interplay of nostalgia and curiosity, we can foster a sense of connection and belonging that fuels our resilience and adaptability.

9

Chapter 9: The Journey of Self-Discovery

The journey of self-discovery is a lifelong process that involves reflecting on our past experiences and exploring new possibilities. By embracing both nostalgia and curiosity, we can gain a deeper understanding of who we are and what drives us. This self-awareness is crucial for building resilience, as it allows us to recognize our strengths and weaknesses and navigate the challenges of the digital age with greater clarity and confidence.

Nostalgia plays a significant role in our journey of self-discovery, as it allows us to reflect on the moments that have shaped our lives. By revisiting our past experiences, we can gain insights into our values, beliefs, and motivations, helping us understand who we are today. This process of introspection enables us to identify patterns in our behavior and recognize areas for growth, ultimately fostering a sense of self-awareness and resilience.

Curiosity, on the other hand, drives us to explore new possibilities and embrace change. By approaching the world with a sense of wonder and inquisitiveness, we can develop a growth mindset that allows us to adapt and thrive in the face of adversity. Curiosity encourages us to question our assumptions and push the boundaries of our comfort zones, ultimately fostering a mindset of growth and resilience.

By embracing both nostalgia and curiosity, we can embark on a journey of self-discovery that helps us build a resilient and adaptable mindset. Nostalgia provides us with a sense of grounding and continuity, while curiosity drives us to explore new possibilities and adapt to change. Together, they create a powerful foundation for growth and resilience, allowing us to navigate the complexities of the modern world with confidence and grace.

10

Chapter 10: The Art of Adaptation

Adaptation is a crucial skill in the digital age, where change is constant and the pressure to adapt is ever-present. By embracing both nostalgia and curiosity, we can develop a mindset that is better equipped to handle the uncertainties of the modern world. Nostalgia provides us with a sense of grounding and continuity, while curiosity drives us to explore new possibilities and embrace change.

Nostalgia helps us build resilience by reminding us of the strength and perseverance we've demonstrated in the past. By reflecting on our past experiences, we can gain insights into our strengths and vulnerabilities, allowing us to approach future challenges with a greater sense of self-awareness and confidence. Nostalgia also fosters a sense of continuity and connection, reminding us that we are part of a larger narrative that stretches across time and space.

Curiosity, on the other hand, drives us to explore new possibilities and embrace change. By approaching the world with a sense of wonder and inquisitiveness, we can develop a growth mindset that allows us to adapt and thrive in the face of adversity. Curiosity encourages us to question our assumptions and push the boundaries of our comfort zones, ultimately fostering a mindset of growth and resilience.

By embracing both nostalgia and curiosity, we can develop the art of adaptation, allowing us to navigate the complexities of the digital age with confidence and grace. Nostalgia provides us with a sense of grounding and continuity, while curiosity drives us to explore new possibilities and adapt to change. Together, they create a powerful foundation for growth and resilience, enabling us to thrive in an ever-changing world.

11

Chapter 11: The Impact of Social Media

Social media has revolutionized the way we connect with others and share our experiences. It provides a platform for us to express our nostalgia and curiosity, allowing us to engage with our past and explore new possibilities. By understanding the impact of social media on our lives, we can harness its potential to build resilience and adaptability.

Nostalgia often finds expression on social media, as we share photos, memories, and stories from our past. These digital mementos allow us to relive the joy and wonder of our experiences, fostering a sense of continuity and connection. By engaging with our digital history, we can draw strength from our past and build a sense of grounding and stability that helps us navigate the challenges of the digital age.

Curiosity, on the other hand, drives us to explore new content and connect with diverse perspectives on social media. The vast landscape of information available at our fingertips encourages us to seek out new ideas and experiences, broadening our understanding of the world around us. By nurturing our curiosity, we can stay ahead of the curve and remain relevant in an increasingly complex world.

Social media also fosters a sense of community and support, as it allows us to connect with others and share our experiences. By engaging with others and embracing different viewpoints, we can create a support network that helps us navigate the challenges of the modern world. Through the interplay of nostalgia and curiosity, social media serves as a powerful tool for building resilience and adaptability.

12

Chapter 12: The Role of Mindfulness

Mindfulness is the practice of being present and fully engaged in the moment. It is a valuable tool for cultivating resilience, as it allows us to navigate the complexities of the digital age with greater clarity and focus. By embracing both nostalgia and curiosity in our mindfulness practice, we can develop a more balanced and resilient mindset.

Nostalgia can enhance our mindfulness practice by helping us reflect on our past experiences and gain insights into our strengths and vulnerabilities. By revisiting our memories with a sense of mindfulness, we can cultivate a deeper understanding of our values, beliefs, and motivations. This self-awareness is crucial for building resilience, as it allows us to recognize our strengths and weaknesses and navigate the challenges of the digital age with greater clarity and confidence.

Curiosity, on the other hand, drives us to explore new possibilities and embrace change in our mindfulness practice. By approaching the present moment with a sense of wonder and inquisitiveness, we can develop a growth mindset that allows us to adapt and thrive in the face of adversity. Curiosity encourages us to question our assumptions and push the boundaries of our comfort zones, ultimately fostering a mindset of growth and resilience.

By integrating both nostalgia and curiosity into our mindfulness practice, we can develop a more resilient mindset that is better equipped to handle the uncertainties of the digital age. Nostalgia provides us with a sense of grounding and continuity, while curiosity drives us to explore new possibilities and adapt to change. Together, they create a powerful foundation for growth and resilience, allowing us to navigate the complexities of the modern world with confidence and grace.

13

Chapter 13: The Art of Reflection

Reflection is a powerful tool for personal growth and development, as it allows us to gain insights into our past experiences and explore new possibilities. By embracing both nostalgia and curiosity in our reflective practice, we can develop a more balanced and resilient mindset.

Nostalgia plays a significant role in our reflective practice, as it allows us to revisit our memories and gain insights into our strengths and vulnerabilities. By reflecting on our past experiences, we can identify patterns in our behavior and recognize areas for growth. This process of introspection enables us to develop a deeper understanding of who we are and what drives us, ultimately fostering a sense of self-awareness and resilience.

Curiosity, on the other hand, drives us to explore new possibilities and embrace change in our reflective practice. By approaching our reflections with a sense of wonder and inquisitiveness, we can develop a growth mindset that allows us to adapt and thrive in the face of adversity. Curiosity encourages us to question our assumptions and push the boundaries of our comfort zones, ultimately fostering a mindset of growth and resilience.

By integrating both nostalgia and curiosity into our reflective practice, we can develop a more resilient mindset that is better equipped to handle the uncertainties of the digital age. Nostalgia provides us with a sense of grounding and continuity, while curiosity drives us to explore new possibilities and adapt to change. Together, they create a powerful foundation for growth and resilience, allowing us to navigate the complexities of the modern world with confidence and grace.

14

Chapter 14: The Influence of Culture

Culture plays a significant role in shaping our experiences of nostalgia and curiosity, as it influences the way we perceive and engage with the world around us. By understanding the impact of culture on our lives, we can harness its potential to build resilience and adaptability.

Nostalgia is often deeply rooted in our cultural experiences, as it allows us to reflect on the traditions, values, and beliefs that have shaped our identity. By revisiting our cultural memories, we can gain insights into our strengths and vulnerabilities, ultimately fostering a sense of self-awareness and resilience. Nostalgia also fosters a sense of continuity and connection, reminding us that we are part of a larger narrative that stretches across time and space.

Curiosity, on the other hand, drives us to explore new cultural experiences and embrace diverse perspectives. By engaging with different cultures and traditions, we can broaden our understanding of the world around us and develop a more inclusive and open-minded approach to life. This openness to new ideas and experiences fosters a sense of adaptability and resilience, allowing us to navigate the complexities of the digital age with greater ease.

By embracing both nostalgia and curiosity in our cultural experiences, we can develop a more resilient mindset that is better equipped to handle the uncertainties of the modern world. Nostalgia provides us with a sense of grounding and continuity, while curiosity drives us to explore new possibilities and adapt to change. Together, they create a powerful foundation for growth and resilience, enabling us to thrive in an ever-changing world.

Chapter 15: The Power of Resilience Resilience is the ability to adapt and thrive in the face of adversity. It is a skill that can be cultivated through the interplay of nostalgia and curiosity, as we learn from our past experiences and explore new possibilities. By developing a resilient mindset, we can navigate the challenges of the digital age with greater confidence and grace.

Nostalgia helps us build resilience by reminding us of the strength and perseverance we've demonstrated in the past. By reflecting on our past experiences, we can gain insights into our strengths and vulnerabilities, allowing us to approach future challenges with a greater sense of self-awareness and confidence. Nostalgia also fosters a sense of continuity and connection, reminding us that we are part of a larger narrative that stretches across time and space.

Curiosity, on the other hand, drives us to explore new possibilities and embrace change. By approaching the world with a sense of wonder and inquisitiveness, we can develop a growth mindset that allows us to adapt and thrive in the face of adversity. Curiosity encourages us to question our assumptions and push the boundaries of our comfort zones, ultimately fostering a mindset of growth and resilience.

By embracing both nostalgia and curiosity, we can develop a resilient mindset that is better equipped to handle the uncertainties of the digital age. Nostalgia provides us with a sense of grounding and continuity, while curiosity drives us to explore new possibilities and adapt to change. Together, they create a powerful foundation for growth and resilience, allowing us to navigate the complexities of the modern world with confidence and grace.

15

Chapter 16: Embracing Change

Change is an inevitable part of life, and it is essential to develop the skills and mindset necessary to adapt and thrive in the face of uncertainty. By embracing both nostalgia and curiosity, we can build a resilient mindset that is better equipped to handle the complexities of the digital age.

Nostalgia helps us build resilience by reminding us of the strength and perseverance we've demonstrated in the past. By reflecting on our past experiences, we can gain insights into our strengths and vulnerabilities, allowing us to approach future challenges with a greater sense of self-awareness and confidence. Nostalgia also fosters a sense of continuity and connection, reminding us that we are part of a larger narrative that stretches across time and space.

Curiosity, on the other hand, drives us to explore new possibilities and embrace change. By approaching the world with a sense of wonder and inquisitiveness, we can develop a growth mindset that allows us to adapt and thrive in the face of adversity. Curiosity encourages us to question our assumptions and push the boundaries of our comfort zones, ultimately fostering a mindset of growth and resilience.

By embracing both nostalgia and curiosity, we can develop the skills and mindset necessary to navigate the complexities of the digital age with confidence and grace. Nostalgia provides us with a sense of grounding and continuity, while curiosity drives us to explore new possibilities and adapt to change. Together, they create a powerful foundation for growth and resilience, enabling us to thrive in an ever-changing world.

Chapter 17: The Future of Resilience As we look to the future, it is essential to cultivate the skills and mindset necessary to navigate the complexities of the digital age. By embracing both nostalgia and curiosity, we can build a resilient mindset that is better equipped to handle the uncertainties of the modern world.

Nostalgia helps us build resilience by reminding us of the strength and perseverance we've demonstrated in the past. By reflecting on our past experiences, we can gain insights into our strengths and vulnerabilities, allowing us to approach future challenges with a greater sense of self-awareness and confidence. Nostalgia also fosters a sense of continuity and connection, reminding us that we are part of a larger narrative that stretches across time and space.

Curiosity, on the other hand, drives us to explore new possibilities and embrace change. By approaching the world with a sense of wonder and inquisitiveness, we can develop a growth mindset that allows us to adapt and thrive in the face of adversity. Curiosity encourages us to question our assumptions and push the boundaries

16

Chapter 17: The Future of Resilience

Curiosity drives us to explore new possibilities and embrace change. By approaching the world with a sense of wonder and inquisitiveness, we can develop a growth mindset that allows us to adapt and thrive in the face of adversity. Curiosity encourages us to question our assumptions and push the boundaries of our comfort zones, ultimately fostering a mindset of growth and resilience.

Nostalgia helps us build resilience by reminding us of the strength and perseverance we've demonstrated in the past. By reflecting on our past experiences, we can gain insights into our strengths and vulnerabilities, allowing us to approach future challenges with a greater sense of self-awareness and confidence. Nostalgia also fosters a sense of continuity and connection, reminding us that we are part of a larger narrative that stretches across time and space.

By embracing both nostalgia and curiosity, we can cultivate the skills and mindset necessary to navigate the complexities of the digital age. Nostalgia provides us with a sense of grounding and continuity, while curiosity drives us to explore new possibilities and adapt to change. Together, they create a powerful foundation for growth and resilience, enabling us to thrive in an ever-changing world.

In the future, resilience will become an increasingly important skill, as the pace of technological advancements and societal changes continue to accelerate. By harnessing the forces of nostalgia and curiosity, we can build a resilient mindset that is better equipped to handle the uncertainties of the modern world. Through the interplay of these powerful forces, we can create a foundation for growth and adaptability, allowing us to navigate the challenges of the digital age with confidence and grace.

Book Description:

In the digital age, where change is constant and the pressure to adapt is ever-present, resilience is more important than ever. "Echoes of Yesterday: How Nostalgia and Curiosity Fuel Resilience in a Digital Age" delves into the dynamic interplay between nostalgia and curiosity and explores how these powerful forces can help us navigate the complexities of the modern world.

Nostalgia roots us in our past, reminding us of our strengths and vulnerabilities, while curiosity propels us forward into the unknown, driving us to explore new possibilities and embrace change. Together, they create a powerful foundation for growth and resilience, allowing us to build a resilient mindset that is better equipped to handle the uncertainties of the digital age.

Through captivating storytelling and thought-provoking insights, this book examines the role of technology, social media, mindfulness, reflection, culture, and connection in shaping our experiences of nostalgia and curiosity. It offers practical strategies for cultivating resilience and adaptability, enabling us to thrive in an ever-changing world.

"Echoes of Yesterday" is a must-read for anyone seeking to understand the forces that drive human resilience and adaptability in the digital age. By embracing both nostalgia and curiosity, we can build a resilient mindset that allows us to navigate the challenges of the modern world with confidence and grace.

www.ingramcontent.com/pod-product-compliance
Lightning Source LLC
LaVergne TN
LVHW020500080526
838202LV00057B/6072